CATHAR RELIGION

Text : Michel ROQUEBERT
Translated from French by : Audrey WAGNER

Editions Loubatières
10 bis, boulevard de l'Europe - 31120 Portet-sur-Garonne
Tél. : 61.72.53.90

RELIGION OF SALVATION

Catharism is a religion of salvation founded on the Revelation. Its Sacred Book is the New Testament. Its prayer is the Our Father. God's messenger, the author of the Book of Revelation, is Christ, and he alone. Salvation is gained through asceticism and baptism. Thus, Catharism is a Christianity ; it never claimed to be anything alse, and even alleged that it was the carrier of the authentic message of Christ to the exclusion of any reference to any other religion whatsoever.

But the interpretation of the Scriptures that the Cathars had was incompatible with Roman orthodoxy. They neither believed in baptism by water nor in the Eucharist nor in any of the sacraments of the Catholic Church. Their Christianity has no redeeming Passion, no Last Judgment, no Resurrection. Their theology, liturgy, moral teachings, rest on dogmatic foundations in complete opposition to those of catholicism. Their dualism, in particular, appeared as a resurgence of Manichaeism — the religion founded in the third century by the Persian prophet Mani. So much so, that in the cradle of Western Christianity this " other " Christianity was looked upon as a foreign body threatening both the dogma and the structure of the official Church — which from the 10th until the 15th century subjected Catharism to the most terrible repression, and eventually succeeded in gaining the upper hand.

HOW CAN WE LEARN ABOUT CATHARISM ?

Catharism is known through three categories of historical source.

First of all, actual Cathars writings. They must have been fairly numerous, but persecutions accounted for the disappearance of most of them. However, two dogmatic treatises and two rituals have come into our hands. One of these treatises, preserved in Florence, is a Latin manuscript from about 1260 which summarizes a lengthy work that the Cathar doctor Jean de Lugio, of Bergame, wrote a short while after 1230 : the Book of the Two Principles. The other, discovered in Prague in 1939, is a copy, still in Latin, of an anonymous treatise composed in the langue d'Oc at the beginning of the 13th century, and whose author was perhaps the " Parfait " Barthélemy from Carcassonne. If

ca er uolontate uiri · si er deo
ur S · Er ubit caro tacta est ·
sr abitauit inobis · Auditur
sr eius · gla diti uni genit ap
re · Plenu gracie ziuitatis ·
ibi testimoniu plibet deipo · e
clamabat dicens · bic est din
ui cpos me uenturus est · a
enne tact est · a pos me par
tar · Er deplenitudine eius n
 souit acce piu gram xpia · ca
er per moisen data est · gla e
tat pilin xpin tacta est ·

ora · echrem nra adu · zauos que
nos prguet · pnor loprire · S ·
d nra anos pdo ·

Adorem deu emanuente tur
himie precar · elas nrar mo
utas greeus ofensios · Aper par
danitr dl paure edlia · edl ouorá ·
S · eperit · edlis onoratu iamb au
ágelin edlis onoratu · S · apostoli ·
Pla oro explate · expla saluatio · d
tuit hditters gliosies crentat · e
dlt bonaurati ourmi· áceioes e
delt tñer emauro eltar · cdñar
nos · S · senlio anos pdner toz go
eñ nos prain · bndicite parcoz dbi ·

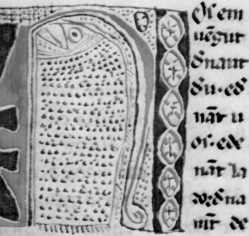

Os em
uegut
dnaut
du·ed
ñat u
os·ed
ñut la
prdna
nit de

Uar moutu soler nres pe
cat elt diti nor orede aui
cadia · piuut experdia · panu
la · redbia cleged cosiuer · abuo
lotat esenes uolotar · Expr p
la nra uolotar · lacti dñat nor
aperta les malignu expiut en
las cars que uestem · bndici
te parcite nobis ·

u glia preceps sunt · expd · e
enedesia · dtuit li nra precar li
auem tant indbes · nupristu m
bratu dl nre nasteñut er si na

Diu ai cula sea parnla
ddu nor conba eli · gñ a

these documents are extremely valuable for learning about dualist theology, the two rituals are none the less so when it concerns the liturgy : the Latin Ritual of Florence as well as the Oc Ritual preserved in Lyon with the complete New Testament translated into " Occitan " for the use of Cathars from the Languedoc. Each document is dated round about 1250. To them must be added a few Apocryphal writings, that is Christian inspired texts used by Cathars but because non-orthodox, had not been kept as canonical Scriptures ; in particular the Vision d'Isaïe (Isaiah's Vision), Ancient Bulgar text used by the Bogomiles, and the " Cène Secrète " (Secret Last Supper), or " Interrogation de Jean " (John's Interrogation), transmitted by the Bogomiles to the Cathars in Italy and in the Languedoc around 1190.

Just as useful are the controversial works by means of which the catholic theologians analysed and attempted to disprove Catharism. More than thirty are known of, written at the end of the 12th and throughout the 13th century, not all of them being of the same importance, and all carrying different values. It would be immature to think that they took pleasure in deforming the religion they were attacking ; these authors themselves warn their readers against cheap slanders and ridiculous accusations which were sometimes directed against Catharism. Only the serious doctrinal points interested them, and these would be discussed keenly, but in general with great intellectual honesty ; especially in the case of the " Liber contra Manicheos " by the former Vaudois couvert Durand de Huesca ; the " Summa quadrapartita ", written in Montpellier by Alain de Lilly or the " Summa adversus catharos " by Moneta de Crémone to quote but a few, not forgetting of course the Summa by the Italian Rainier Sacconi who became a Dominican and an Inquisitor after having been a Cathar Parfait (Accomplished Elder), and who therefore knew more than anyone alse what Catharism was all about.

The last group of documents is from judiciary sources, that is, interrogations conducted by the Inquisition during the best part of a century from 1234 onwards. These were especially plentiful from the Languedoc − nearly 7,000 preserved statements which tell us of over a thousand " Parfaits " and some 40,000 believers in Catharism − these sources are still for the most part unpublished (except for the registers of the Inquisitors Jacques Fournier and Geoffroy d'Ablis). They contain a great deal of information about social life at that time and relive for us the Cathar experience. When it concerns doctrines, beliefs and rites, they tally well with what other sources reveal. In any case one only has to be slightly familiar with these documents to be able. without much difficulty, to detect the pretexts, stratagems, even lies employed by those being interrogated. One of these statements opens up to us the text of the renowned " Pater " (Lord's Prayer) of the Languedoc Cathars : " Payre sant, Dieu dreyturier de bons speritz... " (Holy Father, Legitimate God of good spirits...).

Cruciform window in the Chapel of the Château de Termes in Corbières. Records prove that when Simon de Montfort laid siege to this castle in 1210 and whose Lords were of the Cathar faith, mass had been celebrated there for fifty years.
(Photo Ph. Pons).

THE MYSTERY OF ITS ORIGINS

For forty years, mos tly thanks to the mostly labours of Arno Borst, Jean Duvernoy and René Nelli, historical research, using sources unknown, or those unsufficiently utilised before, considerably improved upon the knowledge of Catharism that we used to have, and even modified this to a great extent. Without necessarily having solved the mystery of its origins, we no longer consider Catharism as the direct descendant of Persian Manichaeism through the intermediary of divers heretical sects such as the Paulicians or the Messalians. If Catharism meets the religion of Mani on specific points, it does not means to say that it descends from it. The conceptual universe of Catharism texts is totally foreign in its vocabulary, in its images and in its myths to that of Manichaean writings. A certain number of fundamental beliefs held by catharism are prior to those of Mani, who certainly drew on these himself while with the Gnostic sects amongst whom he was educated : the idea that there are two opposing creator-principles, that the soul is " Not-created " and being a particle of divine substance is exiled into a wicked world, prisoner of Matter and Time which have forced it to forget its true essence ; the idea that salvation must necessarily go through an initiation by being steeped in an enlightening knowledge ; all that, which is Manichaean and Cathar at the same time, was first of all Gnostic. So much so, that rather than attempt to find hypothetical threads of affiliation, research today turns towards certain streams of primitive Christianity which, without completely being able to be assimilated to Gnosticism, have been able to sustain the influence of gnosis and, in a very special sense, to inflect the reading and interpretation of the New Testament. Similarly, some Church Fathers especially Origène of Alexandria (2nd century) were not unacquainted with the development of the religious system of Catharism.

It must be noted that contemporary research almost takes it for granted that the Bulgarian Bogomilism of the 11th century and the Catharism that the West knew from the 12th to 14th centuries were one and the same religion. Besides, a Bogomile " Pope " from Constantinople, Nicétas, presided at the Cathar Council in 1167 which was held in Saint-Félix-de-Caraman near Toulouse.

FROM THE CATHARS TO THE ALBIGENSES
The Church of the Friends of God

It has been accepted for a long time that the name " Cathare " came from the Greek " Katharos " which means " pure ". Today, this is not quite so evident since it must be pointed out that the Cathars never referred to themselves as such. The term was only employed by their adversaries, and from what we can deduce, was used in a pejorative sense by the German monk Eckbert de Schonau who uttered it for the first time in his sermons in 1163. Thirty-five years later, the Catholic critic Alain de Lille writes that they give them this name from the Latin " catus ", " cat ", because " so it is said, they kiss the hind-quarters of a cat, the form in which Lucifer appears to them... ". An insult which can be explained by the fact that the Cathars, as we shall see, attributed the creation of the visible world to the Principle of Evil, and that in many Mediaeval traditions, notably in Germany, the cat was the symbolic animal of the Devil. From there to spreading it abroad that the Cathars worshipped the Evil Creator in the form of a cat — when in fact they abhorred it — was not a great step, and one that slanderers could negotiate with ease. Besides, it is significant that the mediaeval German word " Ketter " which means heretic comes from " Katte ", " cat ", (in modern German "Ketzer" and Katze).

The dualists were branded with numerous other names : whilst in Germany they were treated as " Cathares ", in Flanders they were called " poplicains " and " piphles ", " patarins " in Italy and in Bosnia, " bougres " or " boulgres " that is " Bulgares " in the North of France, a particularly derogatory expression which ended up as being synonymous with sodomites. But, and without malice this time, they were often called " tisseyres " (weavers) in the Oc region because of their predilection for this trade. Geographical terms were also used : " heretics from Agen, Toulouse, Albi... ". It is this last word, together with that of " Cathares " which had the greatest success, to the extent that it became the equivalent of " Cathar " even when used far away from the Albi region.

The Cathars called themselves "Christians", "good Christians". The ordinary believers willingly called the "Parfaits" "good men", but especially "friends of God", term frequently witnessed in the Languedoc in the 13th century and which is the literal translation of the Slav " bogo-mil ". So that to be absolutely faithful to the vocabulary of that time one ought to call the dualist Church, known as " Bogomile " in the Balkans and " Cathare " in the West, the "Church of the Friends of God".

THE " WORLD " AND THE " KINGDOM "

If there is a dualism of the two Principles it is because catharism is, first and foremost, a dualism of the two Creations. Indeed, the whole system rests upon what is for the Cathars an irrefutable attribute of experience : the existence of two categories of opposing realities.

— on the one hand, spiritual realities, invisible and eternal : this is the Kingdom of the good God, of the " legitimate God ", of the " Living and True God ", of the " God of Justice and Truth ", from whence souls emanate " just as rays emanate from the sun ". This Kingdom is the " new earth and new heaven " which Saint John speaks of in the Book of Revelation, " new ", that is to say " other ", absolutely different in essence from the visible earth and heaven.

— on the other hand, this visible World, an ensemble of material and temporal realities, therefore transitory, doomed to corruption and destruction. It is in this World that Evil appears : flesh and blood knowing suffering, degradation, death ; all vices, all calamities, all evils are linked to the material state. John stated : the World " is set entirely in Evil ".

We could continue citing indefinitely passages from the New Testament quoted by the Cathars in support of this fundamental opposition of the World and the Kingdom : " That which is seen is transient, that which is unseen is eternal ", " Heaven and Earth shall pass, my Word shall remain ", " My Kingdom is not of this World ", " I am not of this World ", etc.

But these two categories of reality are in no way equivalent to each other when set face to face. The Kingdom alone is the absolute Being, for it coincides, so to speak, with God, whose very substance is Love, Charity. As for the World, since it is transient it is vain ; it is, at the extreme, as if it does not exist. For what is the use of existing if it is not forever ? Therefore this World is only Nothingness. Which allows the Cathars to give a metaphysical, abstract interpretation to Saint Paul's phrase " Without charity I am nothing ", there where the catholics only see a simple moral reflection ; the cathars translate it as " Without charity I am nothingness ", which is to say : if I have not within me this particle of divine substance which is to say : if I have not within me this particle of divine substance which is charity, I am reduced to corruptible and vain flesh and blood which only belongs to the World and is consequently Nothingness.

Avignonnet (Haute-Garonne). The Inquisitors Guillaume Arnaud and Etienne de Saint-Thibéry were assassinated there with their retinue in May 1242, by a " commando " of knights and sergeants who descended upon them from Montségur.
(Photo Francis Loubatières).

THE THEOLOGY OF TWO PRINCIPLES

Now the Cathars could not conceive of one Being having been able to create the incorruptible Kingdom where there is no place for Evil, and the transient World where Evil abounds. This then presupposes two distinct and opposing creator-principles.

This fundamental belief of Catharism appeals for three types of argument.

— an argument of pure formal logic taken from Aristotle : " The principles of opposite are opposite. Now, Good and Evil are opposite. Therefore they contain opposite principles ". And to echo this argument, the Cathars quote Saint Matthew's Gospel : " Every corrupt tree bringeth forth evil fruit. A good tree cannot bring forth evil fruit, neither can a corrupt tree bring forth good fruit ".

— a scripturalist argument, that is, taken from the Scriptures, here the third verse of the beginning of Saint John's Gospel : " Per ipsum omnia facta sunt, et sine ipso nihil factum est ". The catholics translate it as : " All things were made by him (God) and without him was not any thing made ", pleonasm challenged by the Cathars. They translate : « Without Him, Nothingness was made ». Which is to say, obviously, the viable World. An interpretation which gave rise in its time to many a controversy in order to ascertain whether the Latin " nihil ", adverb of negation, could also be used as a noun. Not so, said the catholic Doctors. Yes, said the Cathars who found many an example in the New Testament — including Saint Paul's saying quoted above.

But they stumbled over one difficulty : John states that God created Everything ; how then can you imagine another Creation which could have been carried out Without Him — even if it were that of " Nothingness " ? The Cathars replied that Everything does not always have the same meaning in the New Testament : when John states that God created everything, one had to understand by that, the invisibility of totality, the Good Creation (omnia invisibilia) ; but there is also a visible totality (omnia visibilia), which God did not create. The proof is that the Scriptures also say : " All is vanity ". So it cannot refer to the same " Everything ", because God could not have created a vain totality. Therefore there is an Evil Creation, which has its own principle.

— the third argument is of an existential nature ; it is the quasi-visceral refusal — over which no reasoned argument has any sway — to believe that an infinitely good God could have created conditions which allowed Evil to exist, that is, matter and time, in other words the World. For catholics, God being all-powerful, Evil could be a part of his secret design. The Cathars, they somehow invert the hierarchy of divine attributes. Of course, God is allmighty, they say, but in Good alone, because his all-powerfulness is limited by his infinite goodness. Since he is Love, he cannot allow himself, without contradicting or denying Evil.

We must pre-suppose then, separate from God, a creator-principle of the World where Evil happens. This principle is " not-created " and is co-eternal with the good God. But he is not a " True God ". Of course, he is sometimes called the " unknown God ", but he could in no way be considered to be on the same level as the other. He is the Prince of the Prince of the World, the Prince of Darkness, the Wicked Enemy. But he has not absolute existence which belongs only to the True God. He is the negative, corruptive, destructive principle, never the " creator " in the real sense. And his own " creations " must be understood as the permanent experiment of destruction of the Good Creation : confronted with the Spirit, he " invents " Matter so as, by attracting it, he makes the Spirit fall : faced with Eternity he " invents " Time, si that everthing is tainted throughout duration. In brief, his aim is that the Kingdom be destroyed and annihilated in the World. It is a purely "reducing-to-nothingness" force, which, opposed to God, is somehow his reverse-side, but not his equal, neither in value nor in Being.

It was thus that the Cathars perceived the experience of Evil and especially its " weightiness ".

MYTH OF THE FALL

Through his soul, man has characteristics of the Kingdom of the Spirit, of the Good Creation ; through the body he partakes of the World, of the evil Creation. It is, say the Cathars, " the world of confusion ". And this is formed with the help of " the great Perturbation ", that is the Fall, that they expose by means of several Myths. He can be called Satan, Lucifer of the Devil, an emanation from the Principle of Evil come to tempt the Spirits, with the object of injuring the Good God. Some, seduced, agreed to follow him, others fell inadvertently. The Wicked-one then made " tunics of skin " for them in order to imprison them, and it is thus that he threw souls on to the " earth of oblivion " where they no longer knew about their origins nor about their constituent " celestial realities ". Each soul had, nevertheless, left with God its spiritual double, to which the Cathars retain the name of Spirit. It will be seen that salvation was obtained by the reunion of the soul and the spirit.

It was mostly when there were questions concerning the Fall that there were certain divergences at the heart of the Cathar church ; for some, the Devil acted without God being aware : that was absolute Dualism ; for others, he acted with God's knowledge, that was " mitigated " Dualism. When considering the global entity of the system, the difference is relatively secondary, and this dogmatic opposition might well have been just a cover for conflicts of personality. It seems that a large majority of cathars were absolute dualists. Especially so in the case of those from the Languedoc region.

REDEEMING KNOWLEDGE

One can easily accept that salvation for the soul will consist in liberating itself from its fleshly prison, in leaving the World in order to return to the Kingdom. But death, for the Cathars, would not automatically liberate the soul from the body for a Judgment — which in any case they did not believe in — which would send it either to Paradise or to Hell for eternity : there is no Hell other than earth here-below. The soul will not take its place again with God unless, tearing itself away from oblivion, it succeeds in recognising its divine nature, supreme truth which a creature of God, sent by God, came to reveal to man : the Christ. Only the baptism founded by Christ would allow one to gain this knowledge. After which, asceticism would prepare for the soul's liberation. If one had not received baptism or if one was insufficiently prepared, man would see his soul pass into another body. Does not Saint Paul say so himself, that he has already died once ?... This transmigration of souls extended to animals : the Cathars believed that the animal body was also a prison for a fallen celestial spirit ; and the human soul could very well be reincarnated in it.

Redeeming knowledge is of initiatory form : it is a gnosis ; it can only come from the Holy Ghost. The Cathars say in their Ritual that they receive it from Christ himself, with no mediation on the part of the Apostles ; it has been transmitted by the laying on of hands. Infusion of the Spirit by those who already possess it because they themselves have received it is, for the Cathars, the only true baptism ; it is a rite of transmitting knowledge by contact, contrary to the baptism by water that Saint John the Baptist advocated, which is a rite of purification by immersion : it " washes " but it " teaches " nothing. Besides, John the Baptist himself said : " ... But he that cometh after me is mightier than I... he shall baptise you with the Holy Ghost, and with fire... ». And indeed, Christ laid his hands upon others. The Cathars called this " baptism of fire " (as opposed to water), " spiritual baptism ". The symbolism is clear : it was in the form of tongues of fire that the Holy Ghost descended upon the Apostles. They also called it Consolation, " consolament " in the langue d'Oc, " consolamentum " in the Latin texts, because it was the Paraclete or Holy Ghost Comforter that infused knowledge, " l'entendensa del be ", the understanding of Good, the langue d'Oc equivalent of the " Knowledge of Supreme Good " of the Gnostics. Thus a spiritual marriage exists, the mystical reunion of the imprisoned soul in the body with its Spirit remaining in " Heaven ", the soul " receives " its Spirit ; the Spirit comes to seek out its soul, or at least to reveal to it the path it must take to re-join it. If Evil triumphs in Time, only Goodness is able to triumph in Eternity : every soul will free itself, and the whole of (Good) Creation will be saved.

Interrogations carried out by the Inquisitor Bernard de Caux on 13th May and 8th July 1245, of the brothers Jourdain and Aribert, Lords of the Mas-Saintes-Puelles (Aude). (Bibliothèque Municipale, Toulouse, Ms. 609, f° 16). (Photo Lasseube).

et terrandis fratres dni b. et garners et ptes alios de qbus no recolor... e n... ado ibi ...
f. n no recolor de alijs si ado. ut ... in b? credere qd alij ado. quia no ueniebat simul ... ...
et stet ... in ut cta. Jt dix inde buardu de marreuila. z soe. p. te. apd cransu. iy domo ...
uital. et ud ibi cu eis. Aribeum fratres ipis. z et ipis. R. uital. et ... ux ipis. Aim ... ... z
et oms alij ado. ibi deos. te. et stet ... am ut cta. Jt ud terrandi matre z soe. s. te. apd ...
iy domo Wim de canast et udere ibi gerisum z p graua. sem... z ... garmer. filiu dni garmi.
et fler scracia ipis. z uxore buathard? fris ipis. z. et uxore buard barrau z ipe. z. z oms alij.
ado. ibi deos te. et fuit eodem tpe. Jt dix qd ud pater. z soe. s. te. apd mansu z do. ...
de qudero. nepotis ipis. z. et ud ibi ipis bedum de qudero. et Wina matre ipis z ...
et de terra comedebant z deos. z. ado. ibi deos te. f no ud alios. ado. et stet ... in. Jt dix
qd ud bedu de narrica hericu apd mansu iy do. Buf matris dni terei. et inde ibi ptes hoies
extraneos quos no cognouit z godall. quid qu ueneb ibi cu ipo q loq. z ipe. z. et godalh. ado. ibi
deos te. et fuit eode tpe. et dix ipe eriebat de domo dei bi.q. miuent i meto... dom...
septim de bozengar. z p graua semee. Jt dix qd ud duos. te. apud mansu z do. pat...
andreu. et ud ibi. R. graua. et ipe. z. ado. ibi deos te. f no ud deos. R. ado. qa ipe. z.
uenit deus bedum iy dei do. et fuit eode tpe. ydeos te. cre. et bonos hoies. z hie bona
fide. et et uocas et amicos dei. z posse saluari p ipos. z audiuit eos dicentes errores de ...
qd h no fecit eu. et qd hostia sacrata no erat corps xpi. et qd bap?z matmoni no ualebat ad
salute. z qd corpa hoim mozcuoz no resurgent. f ipe no cre. cui ste ipi dicebat. z suos xx. anno
qd hmo cre. te. et bonos. et stet ... anni qd no cre. alibi no ud. te. n ad dedit. n m m ab
eis accepit. et qd dedit eis qda uice flexis. z hec omia fiut oftesso fat ferrario. apd hmoz
...a dix qd ud poncu gray. b. de marre uila. et soe. s. te. et ud ibi cu eis. Jordanu de
qudero. et R. amer. f no ado. n ud ado. et stet ... in. ut cta. z abiurt. te. z nut. ze. b. cognou
cia qd male fecit. qz iq abiut. te. tpz? ...eis. poritsa facta z fut. ... seq. te. z. cre. z
z. cre. z ado. te. z dr frat st garmi. z fr odo. ord pd. z frat. B. Inquisicone le
Jt Aimo et die quo supra. viii. yds Julii. Jordanu dns de marsa z i d. qd ... ud alig... ut abiu...
hericari. Jt dix qd nuq ud. R. garneris cu. te. z. dr hoz st garmi. p. recere ecce de driulha.
fr. R. pelisso. b. hosary. ca. de saluem. z fr. B. Jng...
Jt et die pdeis. Aribert dns del ma. miles. z i d. qd ud ptes hericos z ptes apd mont
securu. f nuq ado. eos ibi. n ud. ado. z stet ... in. Jt dix qd ud garsen matte ipis z. et
buathardam proie ipis z. hericas. apd monte securu. f no ado. eas. n ud. ado. z fuit eos qu
Jt dix qd ud buardu de marre uila. et soe. s. te. apd cransu iy do. Wim uital. et ud ibi
Jordanu ipis. z. z dr godalh. et ipis R. uital. z iy ... z ipe. z. z dr godalh. ado. ibi deos te.
f. flexis genibz. dicendo bne. boni hoies cerate dm y not. f no recolor si ud alios. ado. z stet
... inm ut cta. Jt ud pdeos. te. apd cransu z do. iy iy Wim de Canast. Jumaus. z ud ibi

CHRIST THE MESSENGER

It can be seen that the Christ of the Cathars is very different from that of the catholics. His mission was not redemption. God sent him to convey a message, to reveal the Truth, not to redeem the sins of man by his death.

The Cathars proved to be somewhat uncertain, even contradictory about his exact form. Sometimes they would call him God, one with the Father. Sometimes they would call him God's creature, begotten or adopted Son, in any case later than and inferior to the Father. In brief, the cathars, without doubt, hesitated or faltered over the Mystery of the Trinity.

The same thing regarding the Incarnation. For them, Christ only had a human resemblance, a " fantastic body ", as many passages from the Gospels show, where he had a phantomic consistency of an apparition. Not being really man, he did not really die upon the Cross. The Cathars, nevertheless, respect his apparent Passion, a sort of historical accident, Evil's temporary victory, in Time only, but not in Eternity — and they tell the story of it in their sermons. But they avoid worshipping the Cross, instrument of torture : " If they had hanged your father, they said, would you worship the rope which brought about his death ? "

They gave a purely spiritual and symbolic, never material interpretation of miracles. When Christ healed the blind by touching them with his saliva, it must be understood that by his word he gave them back spiritual insight, not physical eyesight, that is, he rendered them receptive to knowlegde. Likewise the Last Supper : the bread and the wine that he distributed to his disciples were his body and his blood in a purely spiritual sense ; that is, they are his message, this Word with which he is effectively one and the same thing. The Cathars do not therefore believe in a very real presence in the host, and dismiss the Eucharist as being immature idolatry. Which does not prevent them from breaking bread themselves in memory of Christ, but as an act of homage, not as a communion in the catholic sense.

" PARFAITS " AND " BELIEVERS "

Spiritual baptism by the laying-on of hands, the " consolament " is the Cathars's only sacrament. It could only be given to adults, because faith, free choice, clear, conscious, formulated consent, were all necessary : the Cathars dismissed the baptism of young children, who did not understand the meaning of sacrament, as a deviation.

We have seen the function of consolation in the realm of Salvation. Now in order to understand the circumstances in which it was administered, we must realise that, just like Catholicism, Catharism had its ordinary faithful and its ministers.

We call the first, " believers ". The " heretical believers " as the inquisitorial documents make plain. But it was the ministers, the members of the Cathar clergy and they alone who had the right to be called " Christians ", " good Christians ", " good men " or " Friends of God ". It was they whom the Historians would call " Parfaits " or " Parfaites " in the case of a woman. The word is useful, but it must be said that there again, they never used it when referring to themselves. It was the inquisitors who designated as " hereticus perfectus " anyone who had received consolation, that is, " complete heretic " or " accomplished ", without putting into the word " perfectus " the notion of " perfection " such as we understand it. The simple believer never received

consolation except as last rites, in order to " make a good end ". Throughout his life, the frequentation of Parfaits and the teachings he received through their semons, prepared him for it. It was essential, in order to receive it, that a person still had the use of language so as to be able to reply to the officiating minister and to say the prayers. Comatose persons, did not, therefore, receive the consolation. But when persecution or war presented the risk of violent sudden death − as for example during the siege of Montségur in 1244 − believers came to an agreement with the Parfaits in advance, they made their " convenenza " − literally : the pact − that is they pledged to desire consolation if they were mortally wounded ; so in that case the comatose could be " consoled " ; " even if I have lost the use of words but provided I still have a breath of life in me " according to the " convenenza " prescription.

At the same time as being a baptism of the dying and an extreme unction, the consolation was also the sacrament of ordination, when a believer wished to become a Parfait by vocation and whished to receive the sacrament without waiting to be at death's door. He entered a three-year novitiate in a community of Parfaits ; it was both spiritual initiation, an acquisition of dogmatic instruction and a practical preparation for the very restrictive life-style to which

The Château de Montségur (Ariège) : built in 1204, it served as a refuge for the Cathars from the time of the 1209 invasion, then in 1232 it became the seat of the forbidden Church. After its surrender, 225 Parfaits and Parfaites were burnt on 16th March 1244.
(Photo J. Bernadou).

he would be subjected after his ordination, and for the ministry for which he would be responsible : pastoral works of helping believers, preaching, administering the consolation, also manual work, tasks of community life, management of community residence.

In theory, since the ritual was the same, a simple believer who had been " consoled " because he was extremely ill and feared he would die, but who then revived, ought not to return to his former state but continue life as a Parfait. In practics, the Parfaits who " consoled " him did everything to convince him to remain with them, but, if he had no vocation, they did not force him. The " consoled one " who returned to the life of a simple believer, would later on receive another consolation on his death bed. A few cases are known where " consoled ones " let themselves die of starvation if they felt they were getting better, this is the " endura ", which means " fast " in the langue d'Oc. But this suicide was never ritual, it was never imposed by the Cathar Church, contrary to what its enemies, by their malicious accusations, had led people to think for a long time.

The Inquisition, for its part, made no distinction between the consoled and the ordained. Whoever had received consolation was, in its eyes, " hereticus perfectus ", and, by virtue of this, perished at the stake − unless they recanted.

THE LITURGY OF CONSOLATION

It was necessary for the officiating person to be a Parfait, since one had to have received consolation in order to be able to administer it. The ordination took place in the presence of other Parfaits as well as of the parents and friends of the recipient, male or female. The latter would first of all reply to the minister's questions then, after all the Parfaits present had given their consent, he or she would take the vow to follow " the rule of justice and truth ", and " to give himself to God and to the Church of the Good Christians ". Then, if he was married, his spouse would consent by absolving him from all conjugal ties. After an exchange of ritual passages, the candidate could then accept the " tradition " that is, the " Book and Dominical Prayers ", namely the New Testament and the Word of the Lord. He would kneel before a cloth-covered table. The minister would place the New Testament on his head and, together with all the other Parfaits present, would lay his right hand upon it. He would then recite the " Benedicité ", three " Adoremus ", seven " Pater " and three more " Adoremus ". After the reading of Saint John's Gospel he would repeat the " Adoremus " three times more and finish with the words of the Pardon.

When it was a question of consoling a dying person, the state of the invalid sometimes made it necessary to abridge the ceremony. The sick person would receive the sacrament without leaving his bed. During the periods of persecution — which was the case in the Languedoc at the time of the Inquisition, for a century from 1230 onwards — the consolation was given in clandestinity in the presence of only two Parfaits, the officiating minister and his " soci ", that is his companion, brought secretly and generally at night, by devoted agents of the forbidden Church.

WORK AND ASCETICISM

The rules obliged the Parfaits, male and female, to work and to make a living from his or her labour, by virtue of Saint Paul's commandment : " For if any would not work neither should he eat ". Nor was a person of noble origins exempt from this obligation. So, the Parfaits exercised all manner of trades : shoemakers, hatters, tanners, saddlers, carpenters, hawkers, seasonal farmlabourers etc. and very often weavers, with reference to Saint Paul again, who was a tentmaker. In the Languedoc region it was known also that Parfaits were Doctors of Medecine, sufficiently renowned to be retained in the service of any nobility who were of the faith. The women undertook spinning, weaving and especially sewing, making feminine garments, veils, shirts, gloves.

Parfaits and Parfaites had to live and go about in twos as a minimum. They were dressed in black or dark blue from whence the expression " to take the habit " when referring to ordination. The girdle or cord which they tied round their chest was a malicious legend appropriate for making others believe that, on a par with sorcerers, they pratised magic. The men wore beards, at least during the periods when they could, with complete freedom, be distinguished from laymen. Religious observances were very numerous. Cathar asceticism reminds us of the most rigourous monastic rules. But, contrary to what happens in catholicism, it was not only a disciplinary exercise, detaching oneself from the world, the better to serve God. It had a metaphysical value and found its justification in dualism itself.

Firstly, all carnivorous or food of animal origin was strictly forbidden : meat, fat, eggs, milk, butter, cheese. The reasons for this are complex. Christ said " Thou shalt not kill ". So they could not kill animals. There might well be, in every animal, a soul awaiting salvation : its destiny should no be interfered with. In fact, all flesh came about from an act of generation, which was, in essence, diabolical, as we shall see. But fish, a reputedly " cold-blooded " animal, was authorised, just as it was for catholics during Lent or on Fridays.

Parfaits, men and women, were obliged to undergo three periods of abstinence each year, one before Palm Sunday, the second after Whitsun, and the third before Christmas. Thoughout the year they would fast on bread and water on Mondays, Wednesdays and Fridays.

This obvious under-nourishment led to an emaciated pallor that strongly impressed their contemporaries.

Another absolute obligation was continence. It was not a question of celibacy or simple disciplinary chastity : the act of generation was a wicked invention only fit for delaying the liberation of souls. It was in order to multiply " fleshly prisons " that the Evil Principle had created sexual differences and concupiscence. Carnal union was, therefore, essentially Evil and no sacrament could render it licit. Because the catholic church claimed to consecrate it by marriage, the Cathars accused it of acting as a proxy. The observance of this rule was so strict that a Parfait or Parfaite was not allowed to touch, and even had to avoid brushing against, anyone of the opposite sex.

THE RULE OF JUSTICE AND TRUTH

The ordained person, having been brought into a state of justice and of truth by the sacrament of consolation, was obliged to follow the Gospel teachings to the letter with no exception whatsoever.

Oaths were rigorously proscribed (« But I say unto you Swear not at all » — Matthew, 5, 34). Similarly with voluntary untruths, even for a Parfait who had fallen into the hands of the Inquisition and interrogated. Some of them, nevertheless, suceeded in avoiding too explicit a confession, thanks to evasive language and mental reservations. No less absolute was the prohibition of murder. « Thou shalt not kill »), even in cases of legitimate self-defence. This obviously extended to all animals except fish and crustaceans. Refusal to bleed chickens in front of the Inquisitor led many a Parfaite to the stake.

The Cathars refused secular justice (« Judged not, that ye be not judget... »). Together with the proscription of murder, this saying made them defenders of non-violence and adversaries of the death penalty. The believer, guilty of a crime, was ordered, by way of penitence, to let himself be ordained as a Parfait. This was the case of Bélibaste, the last known Languedoc Parfait, burnt by the Inquisition in 1321. Whenever a conflict arose between believers, rather than go before a civil court, they would call upon a Parfait who would arbitrate and settle the affair amicably.

Still, it is worth noting that the Cathars considered cowardice to be a very grave sin, and courage in the face of suffering and death was held to be above all other virtues. The ordained, however, pledged themselves not to be apprehensive, and in particular, not to be afraid of punishment by fire.

Any deviation from the rule was estremely serious because, freed from Evil by the infusion of the Spirit, the Parfait was totally responsible. If he sinned he could not obtain forgiveness except at the end of a long and difficult penitence, and then another consolation was necessary.

As for the simple believer, he, being in the clutches of Evil, was not completely free *not* to sin. It was as if the Devil was sinning within him. He was not subjected to the regulated life-style of the Parfaits. He could have a wife and children ; he could eat meat, go to war, etc. But, of course, he had to have faith, believe in what the Parfaits preached, seek after virtue , prepare himself for the consolation he would receive on his death bed. The Cathar Church would look after him, encourage and help him towards a purification which might awaken in him the desire to become a Parfait in his turn too. In other respects the simple believer had many duties towards the Parfaits' Church. When he met Parfaits or Parfaites, he had to accomplish the rite of " Amélioration ", " melhorer " in the langue d'Oc, " melhoramentum " in Latin, which has become " adoratio " in inquisitorial texts : three genuflexions, each accompanied by a Benedicité, to which one of the Parfaits would reply « May God bless you, make a good Christian of you and lead you to a good end ".

The believer was obliged to listen to sermons, be present at Church ceremonies, which were all public, and which finished up with the ritual Kiss of Peace exchanged with Parfaits, (or with Parfaites in the case of a woman believer). In fact he would often share the Parfaits' meal and the Bread of the Holy Prayer, blessed and broken by the presiding minister, in memory, as we have seen above, of Christ's Last Supper.

THE CHURCH AND CATHAR SOCIETY

The Cathar Church was organised. Did it have a supreme head covering the Cathar Western dioceses and also the Balkan Bogomile churches at the same time ? Divers sources mention a " pope of the heretics ", and Nicetas, in 1167, could well have performed that rôle. But too many indecisions and ambiguities hover over this point for us to be able to settle it decisively, given the actual state of our findings.

On the other hand what is known for certain is that the Church was divided into dioceses. The four Languedoc dioceses were created explicitly in 1167 of Agen, Toulouse, Albi and Carcassonne together with a diocese " of France ". A fifth Languedoc diocese was created in 1226, that of Razes. In Italy we know of the dioceses of Desenzabo, Concorrozzo, Bagnolo, Vicence, Florence, Val de Spolete. In the Balkans, those of Bulgaria, Dragovitia, Melinguia, Dalmatia. Each bishop was assisted by two coadjutors, a Major Son and a Minor Son. On the death of a bishop each coadjutor went up in the hierarchy and a new Minor Son was elected. Then came the deacons, responsible for a more or less extended area of the diocese. Bishops, Sons and Deacons, eighty Cathar dignitaries were known who, in the Languedoc region alone, exercised their ministry during the 13th century.

At the base of the organization were the communities of Parfaits and of Parfaites (separated, of course), called " Houses ", managed by the Elder or the Prior. They were both artisanal workshops and seminaries, where novices were afforded a professional training as well as a moral and dogmatic education which would make them into Parfaits or Parfaites if they proved themselves worthy.

The Parfaits, over and above the obligation to carry out manual labour, had to devote a great deal of their time to prayer, and the men especially, to preaching, during which time they would give meaning to the New Testament for the believers − principally the Gospel of Saint John and the Book of Revelation. More than a thousand Parfaits and Parfaites were known of in the Languedoc in the period between 1200 and 1250. Many of them would go from house to house, devoting themselves to itinerant preaching which could take place anywhere : in a community House, but also in private houses, public squares, fields or orchards. And, during the clandestine period, in woods, attics and thousands of other hiding places.

Every month the community would perform the rite of " Service ", " Apparelhament " in the langue d'Oc. Parfaits and Parfaites would perform an act of submission and confess before the visiting deacon. The believers could attend this. A sermon followed the ceremony which ended with the Kiss of Peace.

It can be seen that Parfaits and Parfaites were the complete opposite to recluses or to those in contemplative orders : their Church would be in permanent contact with the mass of the faithful. The direction taken by the House-Workshops fitted them for total integration into social and economic life. It was certainly an institution, but not in the sense that the Roman Church is one. Unlike the latter, the Cathar Church did not participate in feudal hierarchy, it had no vast lands nor temporal power, it had no fiscal or social claims upon the working-class, nor did it exact tithes or set serfs to work. This could explain much of its success. But if the Parfaits lived very modestly, their Church was rich ; it built up monetary treasures thanks to the products of manual labour and gifts in kind that believers usually donated when they received the consolation of the last rites. The Church used this money to develop the Houses, or put it into circulation by lending it out at interest ; during the time of persecution in the Languedoc, it sent it to Lombardy emigrés, or used it to buy participation in that country and to pay for armed escorts who accompanied the Parfaits who would go clandestinely to administer a consolation. Sometimes the Church would manage believers' funds for them : in this way there was quite a bank − or a savings bak − at Montségur at the time of the famous siege.

Aerial view of the château de Quéribus in the Corbières. It served as a refuge for the Cathar bishop Benoît de Termes, and did not fall into the hands of the Royalist troops until 1255, eleven years after Montségur, (Photo M. Roquebert).

THE IMPLANTATION OF CATHARISM

Whether it was called Bogomilism, Patarinism or Catharism, the dualist religion, witnessed from the 10th until the 15th century, leaned towards universality. It was a European fact.

The country in which it had been established the longest was Bulgaria, where a " pope " named Bogomil preached about the year 950. Was it his real name, the Bulgarian equivalent of the Greek " Théophile " ? Or was it a sobriquet for being head of the Church of the Friends of God ? Nothing much is really known about it. In any case, from Bulgaria Bogomilism reached Dragovitie (Western Macedonia), the Mélinguia (Peleponnese) ; to the East, Philadelphia in what is now Turkey ; to the West, Dalmatia and Bosnia. At the end of the 12th century, the " ban " of Bosnia, Kulin, even proclaimed it as the State religion. The crusade conducted by the king of Hungary on the orders of the Papacy did not prevent it from remaining so. Bogomilism did not disappear from the Balkans until the Turkish conquest, which started in 1463 and ended in 1481.

Although Bogomilism spread from the Balkans thanks to itinerant preachers who took the great trading routes — Pô valley, Rhône valley, Rhine valley — it does not mean to say that there were no spontaneous centres of dualism that sprung up in the West. A first " heretical " wave was felt in the first third of the 11th century : Vertus in Champagne about the year 1000, Toulouse in 1017, Orleans in 1022, Monteforte in Italy in 1034. From 1050 until 1100 there was a marked decline, which coincided with the success of the Gregorian reforms. But everything started up again stronger than ever from 1100, and it could be said that the 12th century was the " golden age of heresy " : Antwerp, Louvain and Bruges from 1110 to 1115, Soissons in 1114, Utrecht in 1135, Liège in 1135 and 1144, Toulouse and the Albigeois in 1145, Oxford in 1160, Cologne and Besançon in 1163, Trêves in 1164, Vézelay in 1167, Arras in 1172, Rheims in 1180, Troyes in 1200, London in 1210, Strasbourg in 1211, etc. Meantime, as we have seen, Catharism was organised into dioceses in the county of Toulouse and the viscountcy of Carcassonne and was solidly established in Lombardy and Central Italy. Later, crossing the Pyrenees, it reached Catalonia and Northern Aragon.

Remains of the Château de Minerve (Hérault). (Photo Francis Loubatières).

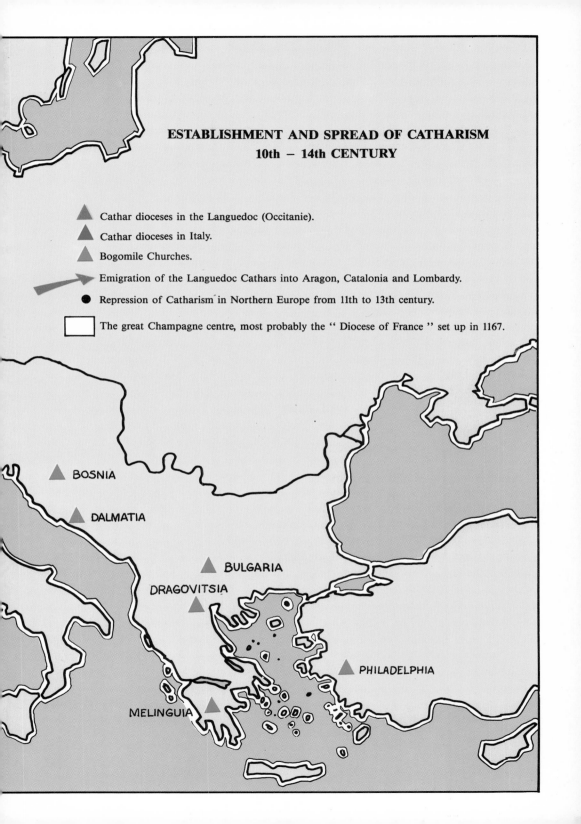

ESTABLISHMENT AND SPREAD OF CATHARISM
10th – 14th CENTURY

▲ Cathar dioceses in the Languedoc (Occitanie).

▲ Cathar dioceses in Italy.

▲ Bogomile Churches.

→ Emigration of the Languedoc Cathars into Aragon, Catalonia and Lombardy.

● Repression of Catharism in Northern Europe from 11th to 13th century.

☐ The great Champagne centre, most probably the " Diocese of France " set up in 1167.

BOSNIA

DALMATIA

BULGARIA

DRAGOVITSIA

PHILADELPHIA

MELINGUIA

THE REPRESSION :
CRUSADE AND INQUISITION

Very soon the Church of Rome alerted the secular authorities so that they might impede the rise of a religion which both opposed official dogma and threatened the structure and institutions of this same Church : the Cathars, obviously, did not pay any tithes to the Devil's Church, for, worshipping the God of Genesis, it was thus worshipping the creator of the visible World.

There where the authorities were hand-in-glove with Rome, repression was terrible : the dates quoted above are, for the most part, those of hangings or martyrdom at the stake. But where feudalism and urban consulates refused to associate themselves with repression, Catharism could develop almost freely and institutionalise itself in its turn. Apart from Bosnia, this was the case in the Lombardy towns as well as the Languedoc. There, it was no longer a matter of " sects " being delivered up to torture immediately after appearing and being located, but of a real Counter-Church which was openly opposed to Rome, it was organising itself and had its own economic and social structures. In a word, a whole new system which threatened to replace the established order.

The repression of Catharism in the Languedoc was a great tragedy : the extent of the undertaking even had political repercussions which were given great prominence in the history books of the Oc region and of France, because at that time, much more naturally drawn towards Barcelona than Paris, the whole of the languedoc region was delivered up to the Capetian Crown. Responding to the wishes that Pope Innoent III had held since 1198, the " Crusade against the Albigeois " set out in 1209. For nine years the Northern Barons led by Simon de Montfort ravaged the country " by fire and by sword " burning Parfaits and Parfaites at the stake and also massacring populations without discrimination of religion, confiscating the conquered lands for their own ends. A catholic prince intervened against them : Peter II, king of Aragon, count of Barcelona. He was killed in 1213 at the battle of Muret, and Simon de Monfort was proclaimed count of Toulouse by Rome.

From 1216 to 1224 the Languedoc overlords conducted a war of liberation which enabled them to take back all their lands ; and Catharism returned to its former state. But King Louis VIII's crusade in 1226 sparked off the irreversible defeat of the Languedoc princes, ratified in 1229 by the Treaty of Paris

In the pentagram (hollowed-out or natural ?) of Bethléem caves at Ussat (Ariège), a man can stand upright with outstretched arms. According to tradition the Cathars attributed a symbolic meaning to it, for small stone, terra cotta and lead pentagrams have been discovered at Montségur, at Lastours and at Ussat. For the Ancients and the Alchemists, this geometrical figure symbolises wisdom and knowledge.
(Photo René Gailli).

which sanctionned the conquest and the annexation. Then the Inquisition took over from the Northern nobility in the hunting down of Parfaits and Parfaites. It required a whole century to track down, capture and put them to death at the stake one by one, to dismantle their Church, eradicate from hearts and minds the religion of the Two Principles. But catholic action was also spiritual. Having been created for the needs of the cause, the mendicant orders of Dominicans and Franciscans, by proposing to men of good faith an apostolic life-style that beforehand they could only have found in Catharism, gave them the possibility of " making a good end " without leaving the Roman Church. In Italy too, Catharism ended by dying out in the 14th century due to the combined effects of inquisitorial violence and the attraction of the recently introduced convents of friars.

So, the West had received a very profound message through faith and morality preached by the Church of the Friends of God. It was very hard, very exacting. Many a time History had judged it as being too pessimistic to have had any real chances of survival. But it was a great message of love, and, on many counts, of tolerance and freedom. It is not just by chance that the world of today bows down with such strong emotion before the ashes of this martyrized religion.

Rising out of the mist the " Pog " of Monségur silhouetted below the Ariège hills.

TO FIND OUT MORE...

Cathar texts : René NELLI : " Ecritures cathares ". *Planete,* 1968. Complete Cathar writings translated into French.

The Religion : Jean DUVERNOY : " Le catharisme ", volume I : " La religion des cathares " ; volume II : " Histoire des cathares ". *Privat,* Toulouse, 1976 and 1979. Re-published 1986.

René NELLI : " Le phénomène cathare ". *Privat,* Toulouse, 1964.

La vie quotidienne des cathares du Languedoc au XIIIᵉ siècle. *Hachette,* 1969.

La philosophie du catharisme. *Payot,* 1975.

Déodat ROCHE : " Le catharisme ". *Cahiers d'Etudes Cathares,* Narbonne, 2 vol., 1973 and 1976.

Jean DUVERNOY, Paul LABAL, Robert LAFONT, Philippe MARTELL, Michel ROQUEBERT : " Les cathares en Occitanie. *Fayard,* 1981.

CAHIERS DE FANJEAUX N° 3 : " Cathares en Languedoc ". *Privat,* 1969.
N° 20 : " Effacement du catharisme ". *Privat,* 1985.

The National centre of Cathar studies (Villeghy, 11600 Conques/Orbeil. Tel. : 68.77.10.21) publishes a quarterly magazine on mediaeval heresiology : " Hérésis ".

Dimitre ANGELOV : " Le bogomilisme en Bulgarie ". On Bogomilism. Translated from the Bulgarian. *Privat,* 1972.

Michel ROQUEBERT : " L'épopée cathare ", 1209-1229. On the Crusade against the Albigeois. Three Volumes. *Privat,* 1970, 1977 and 1986.

For the younger reader : — cartoon form :
" Aymeric et les cathares ". *Ed. Loubarières,* Toulouse, 1978.
" Aymeric à Montségur ". *(Id.* 1981. Text by Michel Roquebert, Drawings by Gerald Forton.

© Loubatières Editeur

Achevé d'imprimer sur les presses des imprimeries Fournié à Fonsegrives 31130 Balma en mai 1991

Dépôt légal 2ᵉ trimestre 1991

ISSN 0298-024 X — ISBN 2-86266-032 – 9